The Crystal Healing Bible

The Ultimate Guide to Crystals for Healing and Protection

Table of Contents

Introduction	**6**
Chapter 1: Understanding the Basics of Crystal Healing	**7**
What Are Crystals?	7
Shapes of Crystals	8
Health Benefits of Crystal Healing	9
Relieves Headaches	10
Improves Sleeping Difficulties	10
Improves Low Energy	11
Increases Libido	11
Improves Focus Difficulty	11
Improves Mental Clarity	11
Chapter 2: Types of Crystals for Crystal Healing	**13**
Chapter 3: How to Do Crystal Healing	**32**
Placing Crystals on the Chakras	32
How to Clear Your Crystals	34
Mind Programming	36
Conclusion	**37**

Introduction

Crystals have long been used since the ancient times for healing. Each crystal is characterized of having unique internal structure that creates a certain frequency. The frequency that crystals give is said to produce healing abilities and using them in a correct way can help restore the balance in the body.

Crystal healing has been practiced by our ancestors. The first ever recorded historical reference of crystal therapy dated back during the ancient Sumerians. Another civilization that uses crystals for healing is the ancient Egyptian. Ancient Egyptians used emeralds, lapis lazuli and turquoise and carved amulets out of them. The thing is that all civilizations and tribes have some sort of beliefs about the ability of crystals to heal.

Today, crystal healing has a lot of followers and this is the reason why there are many books and references available about this particular subject. In fact, it is no longer viewed as part of alternative culture but has now found its way in mainstream complimentary therapy. If you are interested in crystal healing, then this book is definitely for you.

Chapter 1: Understanding the Basics of Crystal Healing

Crystal healing is a non-invasive and gentle type of alternative healing. It is used in holistic medicine to provide harmony to the body, mind, emotions, and spirit so that we will have increased feelings of well-being and positivity. This chapter will discuss about the basics of crystal healing.

What Are Crystals?

Crystals are minerals formed by the earth. They take on interesting three-dimensional shape due to the unique and repeating patterns of their atoms. The appearance of crystals depends on their intrinsic characteristics as well as the conditions which they were formed. This is the reason why some crystals take very unique shapes and it makes it very easy for you to identify one crystal from the other due to their crystal habit.

The repeating structure of crystals is believed to have invested memories or energies. This means that you can program crystals to hold any kinds of energies – both positive and negative – that you want. Its ability to store memories and energies is also the reason why it is important that you cleanse crystals all the time because it can pick up any strong energy that surrounds it.

Shapes of Crystals

Different crystals come with various energetic properties. While many people associate the properties of crystals to its color and transparency, many experts believe that the shapes of crystals can affect its qualities. Below is the list of the available shapes of crystals used in crystal healing.

- **Chunks:** Chunks refer to the crystals without any notable facets. This shape is used for enriching rooms or individuals. It is also used in meditation as it has the ability to collect negative energy from air.

- **Single terminated wands:** Crystals that take on this shape have a rounded or rough edge at one point and tapers off to the other. This crystal has an ability to focus on healing, meditation and cleansing.

- **Clusters:** Clusters refer to an aggregate of small crystals that have formed a mass together. The clusters are great in enriching the workplace or home. They can use to invigorate, cleanse and provide calm atmosphere.

- **Tumblestone:** Tumblestones are tiny stones or crystals that have been tumbled with an abrasive material thus its sides have become shiny and smooth. People carry tumblestone in their pockets to give them energy throughout the day.

- **Cut crystals:** Cut crystals are those that have been cut and polished to form artificial shapes like spheres or pyramids. Aside from being attractive, the various shapes of crystals have different functions.

Health Benefits of Crystal Healing

Crystal healing is used most often for its health benefits. Crystals can provide positivity to the mind, body and spirit and this is the reason why many people carry crystals as part of their jewelry to be able to have more energy during the day. Below are the health benefits of crystal healing.

Relieves Headaches

Crystals can be used to provide relief to people suffering from headache. However, the crystals used to treat headache largely depends on the cause of the headache. For instance, if you are having a headache due to tension and stress, you can put in the affected part crystals like amber, amethyst, and turquoise. If you are suffering from migraine, you can use lapis lazuli in combination with amethyst to relieve the symptoms. Lastly, if the cause of headache is due to the imbalance in the chakra energy of the head and solar plexus, then using moonstone or citrine is your best option.

Improves Sleeping Difficulties

People who have trouble sleeping can benefit from crystals. Again, the type of crystals that should be used depends on the reason for troubled sleeping. If you cannot sleep because of worry, then you can place under your pillow rose quartz, chrysoprase, amethyst or citrine. If your restlessness is caused by overeating, then using iron pyrite or moonstone can help calm your stomach. Tourmaline can be used if you are having trouble sleeping due to nightmares.

Improves Low Energy

Crystals that are naturally red, yellow or orange can help improve our energy levels. Examples of crystals that can improve your levels of energy include golden amber, red garnet or yellow topaz. You can also use tiger's eye, japer and citrine placed on the solar plexus to boost your energy.

Increases Libido

Men who suffer from low libido are often emotionally strained. The negative emotions that they feel can totally block their sexual energies. To improve the libido, using crystals like fluorite as well as garnet can ignite the passion again.

Improves Focus Difficulty

People who find it difficult to focus can benefit from quartz to give mental clarity and carnelian which clears extra thoughts.

Improves Mental Clarity

Crystals are believed to promote mental clarity by dissolving the blockage of our emotional expression. If you are going to use crystals, make sure that you wear it around your neck for healing effect. Crystals that give mental clarity usually take on the green color. Examples of such crystals include jade, and emerald. Cool-colored crystals like rose quartz, opal and blue lace agate as they help detoxify the emotions.

Chapter 2: Types of Crystals for Crystal Healing

Crystals have effective albeit mysterious powers to heal the mind, body and soul as well as provide protection. There are many crystals that you can use in order to achieve the effects that you desire. This chapter will discuss about the types of crystals used in crystal healing.

Abalone
Abalone is technically not a crystal because it is a type of shell obtained from the sea. However, ancient people believed that it holds a great deal of energy. Its smooth and shiny interior can invoke calm demeanor. The rainbow pastel sheen on the abalone shell enhances feelings of beauty, love, peace and compassion. It is also excellent if you need relationship guidelines.

Abalone shell is also a great gift for those who survived traumatic experiences to let them know that they their true beauty shines through. After all, the abalone only became beautiful because it was tossed around under the sea for a long time.

Abalone also improves the immune system and aids in the distribution of proteins thus it can be used by athletes for improved stamina and strength.

It can influence the solar plexus, heart and throat chakras. It is good for those with astrological signs of Cancer, Aquarius, Pisces and Scorpio.

Agate
Agate is considered as one of the oldest types of healing stones. It carries a lot of energy and is used in achieving balance and stability.

Agate is believed to improve the conditions of the blood vessels, stomach, eyes, bones, skin, uterus and the lymphatic system. It can also help improve the analytical abilities of individuals while reducing anger bitterness and trauma. Overall, agate can provide calming and soothing effects that can improve confidence, concentration and self-acceptance.

This stone is perfect for Gemini. It affects different types of chakras depending on its color. It is interesting to take note that agate comes in a variety of color from brown to blue.

Amethyst

Amethyst is considered as a natural stress reliever. It is characterized of having a deep or light purple color. It is a very powerful crystal that is used to heal and protect people. The healing energy of amethyst allows it to transmute the lower vibrations to high frequencies thus it has the ability to transform negative energies to love.

Amethyst activates the crown chakra thus allowing access to the divine. It also clears and repairs holes in the aura so that divine energy can easily be drawn in.

It is used in treating many physical ailments like acne, burns, bruises, cancer, eczema, headache, memory loss, metabolic problems, skin irritation, lack of sleep and itching to name a few.

It can also relieve emotional issues like anger, balance, fear, grief and anxiety. It helps restore the emotional balance of its users.

Aquamarine
Aquamarine resonates the clean energy of the ocean thus providing calm and protection during traveling. It also provides balance to our emotions as well as improves the personal power.

Aquamarine connects and activates the heart chakra thus allowing one to realize their truths thus encouraging self-expression. It also opens the third-eye and throat chakra that support seeing the truth and expression.

This crystal helps treat different conditions like acne, allergies, bladder problems, edema, eye problems and everything related to the neck and head.

It also provides mental clarity, calmness, composure and coping attitude during crisis.

Aventurine
Aventurine is a stone that is used to clear EMF smog as well as other pollutants present in the environment. This is really important for people suffering from geopathic stress. Aventurine also helps stabilize the mind from things that are chaotic.

As the name implies, aventurine helps open your mind to try new things and possibilities. It is also the stone that improves your creativity. This crystal affects your brains and muscles.

Azurite
Also dubbed as the "stone of the heaven", this royal blue-colored crystal has awakening psychic abilities in

helping us recognize our intuition. It also helps us in relieving our worries, phobias and nagging negativities.

Azurite also infuses logic with love thus enforcing compassion with others. It opens the throat chakra thus encouraging communication from the heart. It can also dissolve blockage and helps relieve mental stress.

Black tourmalinated quartz
Black tourmalinated quartz is formed with the aggregation of black tourmaline and quartz. It provides luck and wealth. When worn, it produces a large amount of light to encapsulate the body which can unblock negative energies to create overall balance in the body.

Bloodstone
Bloodstone is considered as a powerful stone that can heal many ailments. It is composed of green chalcedony and small red jasper.

It is used to purify the body from all negative energies. It also brings love in any situation especially those that are surrounded by negative energies. It can enhance the mind and bring clarity to the mind.

It can help detoxify the liver, spleen and kidneys. It can also benefit all blood rich organs as it regulates the blood flow. It affects the root chakra as well as the heart and solar plexus chakra.

Carnelian
Carnelian, during the ancient times, is used to protect the dead in their journey to the afterlife thus this gem helps people who have great fears about death.

Carnelian opens and activates the sacral chakra thus increasing the physical energy. It also promotes courage, creativity and compassion.

It can help treat physical symptoms such as improved blood circulation, male impotency, improve the appetite and boost the functions of the liver, bladder and spleen.

Carnelian also improves the mental capabilities by allowing one to experience deep meditation and concentration. The strong energy in carnelian keeps out unnecessary thoughts thus making people better at decision making.

It is also a good in protecting one from accident and it can be placed inside homes to protect your property from storm damage, fire and theft.

Chrysocolla

Chrysocolla is a crystal that invokes peace. It provides calmness in times of stress. Unlike other gemstones, it gently collects negative energies thus it does not overwhelm its users.

It is a good support stone with quartz. It can improve creativity, self-awareness and inner balance. Using it when one feels anger and guilt brings out the best effects.

Chrysocolla opens and activates the throat chakra thus encouraging wise communication. It also affects the heart chakra to help people seek the truth and the third eye chakra to enhance meditation and intuition.

The chrysocolla can also be used to guard homes against obnoxious neighbors and unwanted visitors. It is a great crystal for elderly people as it eases feelings of living alone.

Physically, this gemstone can help treat ailments involving the back, stomach and lungs. It also helps improve rheumatism and painful joints.

Chrysoprase

Chrysoprase helps connect with altruistic feelings for the family. It opens and activates the heart chakra for the Chi to flow through the body.

This crystal is considered as the stone of compassion and grace and it facilitates deep meditation as well as relaxation. It can be used to encourage acceptance and it can banish feelings of both superiority and inferiority. Carrying a small stone of chrysoprase in the pocket can help one release bitterness and fear all throughout the day.

The physical symptoms that can be alleviated from chrysoprase include disorders involving the heart. The lemon-colored chrysoprase, citron, is used to assimilate vitamin C and increase fertility.

Citrine
Citrine provides a joyful vibration to help people overcome depression and learn effective communication skills. It can activate the imagination and bring more creative visions in a clearer mind.

Citrine also encourages optimism and wearing it can bring more positive outlook in life. Powered by the sun, this crystal cleanses as well as energizes. It activates the solar plexus chakra.

It can treat physical symptoms involving the digestive system, metabolism and spine. Citrine can also help detoxify the circulation thus improving conditions of fatigue.

Clear quartz
Clear quartz activates the energy centers in the body. It is also very powerful in energizing the body. Quartz also helps wearer think with clarity thus allowing him or her to become more focused on achieving their dreams and desires.

Coral
Coral is made up of Calcium carbonate and it can take on different colors like red, gray, black and blue. Coral helps balance the emotions and absorbs negative emotions thus relieving people from depression. It is a soothing and protective stone that taps the ancient knowledge in learning the spiritual tradition.

Due to its hard characteristics, corals alleviate the weaknesses in the bones thus helping people suffering from osteoporosis and other brittle bone diseases. They can also help people who are suffering from carpal tunnel syndrome and other diseases in the skeletal system.

Freshwater pearl
Pearls are used in ancient times to bring life, love and beauty. Pearls also make individuals become more

conscious about their problems so that they can have focus when it comes to solving problems. Pearls are also linked to innocence thus allowing one to see life through the eyes of compassion.

Garnet
Garnet symbolizes heat and fire and it inspires brightness that illuminates dark places and souls. Since it provides light, garnet is a great stone for treating depression as it brings in joy and warmth.

The fire characteristics of garnet stimulate the survival instinct and courage in any pressing situation. It can bring internalized ideas in an instant.

The crystal garnet cleanses the chakras of negative energies and re-energizes them. It is used to activate and balance the sacral chakra as well as sex drive. Its ability to improve the sex drive inspires love and passion.

Goldstone
Goldstone s a man-made glass that is infused with copper particles as well as cobalt, chromium and manganese. The sparkles of goldstone are reminiscent of a starry night sky.

Goldstone is a good deflector of bad energies and it also provides protection. It can stimulate the nervous system by transmitting healing energies. It allows long-distance healing.

This gemstone helps alleviate conditions like migraine and eye ailments.

Hematite
Hematite absorbs the negative energies around you. It is a very protective stone and it can help people stay grounded under different situations. Hematite activates the root chakra thus transforming negative energies into positive vibrations.

It also aid in providing high spiritual energy thus aiding people in their spiritual journey. When it is carried in the pocket or as worn as a form of jewelry, it provides equilibrium and self-confidence.

Hematite can help protect people against geopathic stress and it can also help improve the blood and liver thus its name.

Jade
In Chinese traditions, jade is considered as a powerful lucky charm. There are different types of jade which include jadeite and nephrite.

Jade usually exists as a green-colored gem but it can exist in different colors which include pink, white, lavender, yellow, red, black, orange and blue.

This gemstone brings in harmony and cohesiveness in the family and at work. It also helps strengthen the relationship especially those who are recovering loss or separation.

Jade is also used in treating the disorders related to the male reproductive system. It can also be treated to repair cells and bones and it also helps regulate blood pressure.

Jasper
Jasper is dubbed as the "supreme nurturer" as it sustains stability in times of stress. It also helps facilitate dreaming and protects the person while dreaming by absorbing negative energies.

Jasper also has the ability to balance and align the mental, physical and emotional bodies with the etheric realm. Moreover, it also promotes courage and determination, creativity and imagination.

Labradorite
Labradorite is a crystalline form of feldspar. It gives off flashes of colors when polished. This highly mystical

gem improves the intuition as well as the psychic abilities thus it activates the third eye chakra.

It balances the intellect and intuition and dispels illusions. Labradorite is very protective against negative energies by sealing the aura from all energy leaks where negative energies can get through.

Labradorite enhances strength and the feelings of self-worth. It is also used in healing painful old memories and prepares the body for ascension.

Lapis lazuli
Lapis lazuli is made from a combination of different minerals which include calcite, lazurite and pyrite. It opens and balances the throat chakra thus promoting full communication. It also encourages truthful expression when it comes to sharing information with others.

Aside from opening the throat chakra, lapis lazuli also opens the third eye chakra which allows you to connect your physical self to the celestial kingdoms thus helping you achieve spiritual attainment. It also provides protection against psychic attack by shielding the negative energies and vibrations around you.

Lapis lazuli helps improve the immune system as well as the thyroid and brain function.

Malachite

Malachite is considered as the stone of transformation and it functions in cleansing all chakras in the body. It also promotes abundance and intention.

This stone absorbs the energy and draws emotions towards the surface. It opens and activates the throat and heart chakra.

Malachite has the powerful ability to amplify all types of energies thus it should only be used in positivity. It is also used in opening the third eye to facilitate the psychic vision.

Physically, malachite has an equalizing and balancing capacity that helps protect the body from radiation. It is also used to treat inflammation like asthma, swollen joints, arthritis and broken bones.

Moonstone

Moonstone is closely associated with the moon thus its name. Considered as the stone of insight and intuition, moonstone helps balance our emotions thus it has a soothing effect.

Moonstone activates the sacral, crown and third eye chakras which connect us to the divine inspiration.

Since it enhances our emotions, it has the ability to treat depression and clarifies our judgment.

Moonstone can also promote the reproductive and digestive system. It also helps promote better sleep for jetsetters.

Mother of pearl
Mother of pearl is the iridescent lining inside shells of certain mollusks. It is associated with the element of the ocean thus it has powerful healing energy.

It holds a pure energy that can keep the evil away. It is also known to help reduce fear and promote prosperity thus allowing you to become more positive in life.

Obsidian
Obsidian is a volcanic glass that ranges from black to mahogany, red and green brown in color. It is a powerful grounding stone that activates the root chakra which is associated with the Earth.

When used incorrectly, it can release undesirable negative energies that can cause trauma. However, if used properly, it can protect the wearer against hostilities.

Obsidian can help treat diseases at the roots by clearing the blockage thus it is used in detoxifying the body.

Onyx

Black onyx provides protection by absorbing negative energy and transforming it into something good. It aids in the development of physical and emotional strength as well as stamina.

Onyx stimulates clarity in the mind thus fostering wise decision-making to its users. Since it is a powerful protection stone, it is used by people who are suffering from nightmares.

Peridot

Peridot is a crystal that activates the heart and solar plexus chakra. It has a lot of positive energy which is beneficial among people who are currently suffering from traumatic experiences.

It also has the ability to bring out unconditional love thus making it a perfect gift for parents to their children. To maintain peaceful relationship with others, it is crucial to wear peridot at all times.

This gem produces powerful healing vibrations that can affect the body as a whole. It can provide healing to the lungs, stomach and heart. It is also used to assist natural childbirth.

Pyrite

Pyrite is a rock with highly protective powers. It has the ability to shield the users from all types of negative energies by mending tears in the aura.

If you carry a pyrite in your pocket, it can protect you from physical dangers. It activates all chakras in the body thus enhancing the mind, body and soul of individuals.

It can purify the body and can help increase vitality during times of stress. Moreover, it balances the energy fields thus allowing you to easily recover from stress.

Rhodonite

Rhodonite has the ability to balance the emotion as it activates the heart chakra. This also makes this crystal great for attracting love and dispelling negative energies.

Rhodonite is also used in meditation as it promotes peace on the wearer's physical journey. It can also help the wearer discover his or her passion and learn new skills to enhance such passion.

It is also believed to heal and detoxify the liver, heart, lungs and the nervous system. It is also used to stimulate the metabolism and reduce anxiety.

Rose quartz
Rose quartz is the stone that symbolizes unconditional love. It is one of the most important crystals that you need to have in order to have good relationship with your family and friends.

It also as a soothing effect and it fosters reconciliation and empathy as well as lower stress and tension. Putting a piece of rose quartz near the bedside can improve the relationship corner.

It is also used to treat diseases of the hurt and lungs. Moreover, people suffering from vertigo, anxiety and asthma can take advantage of the calming effects of rose quartz.

Selenite
Selenite is a crystal that is used for energy clearing. It has the ability to protect, clear and shield your energy body. Selenite crystals also have the ability to magnify the energy of other gemstones that are placed on top of it thus making recharged with a lot of positive energy.

In holistic medicine, selenite is used in treating diseases like cancer and tumor reduction.

Turquoise

Turquoise is said to create a bridge between heaven and earth. Many Native American believe that it is a master healer. It activates the throat chakra which fosters honesty and open communication. It also helps align the chakras thus strengthening the body.

Chapter 3: How to Do Crystal Healing

Proponents of crystal healing believe that crystals have properties and energies that can facilitate healing of different diseases. In this particular alternative treatment, the gemstones are assigned different properties which were already mentioned in the previous chapter. This chapter will discuss how to do crystal healing.

Placing Crystals on the Chakras

In a treatment session, crystal healing involves the healer placing different types of crystals on the body. The position of the crystals refers to the different chakra points. The healer use stones based on the symptoms that their patients have indicated. This section will discuss about the seven chakras in crystal healing.

- **Crown chakra:** The crown chakra is located on top of the head. Place a violet crystal or a clear quartz stone in this area so that it will balance and integrate the mental, physical, emotion and spiritual state of the patient. Placing a crystal in this location can also promote positive patterns and thoughts.

- **Brow chakra:** This chakra is located in the center of the forehead and in between the brows. This is activated by any indigo or dark blue crystal. This chakra promotes intuitive skills and better memory. It also promotes self-knowledge.
- **Throat chakra:** Once activated, this chakra brings open communication, self-expression and peace. Place only light-blue crystals in this area.
- **Heart chakra:** The heart chakra is activated by any green crystal. It is located at the center of the chest therefore it promotes calm and a sense of direction. You can also add a pink stone in this chakra for effective emotional clearing.
- **Solar plexus chakra:** Solar plexus chakra is located between the navel and the ribcage. It is activated by any yellow crystal. Once activated it can help reduce anxiety and promote confidence.
- **Sacral chakra:** Sacral chakra is located in the lower abdominal area. Placing an orange crystal in this area can balance creativity as well as help release all blockages in your life so that you can enjoy and live your life to the fullest.
- **Base chakra:** The base chakra is located at the base of the spine and in between the legs.

Placing a red or black crystal in the area can balance physical energy and increase motivation as well as practicality.

When placing the crystals in the body, make sure that you are lying down. To get the right balance of energies, make sure that all of the crystals are aligned with each other and that you are using the appropriate colored stone for each chakra. It is also necessary to place a quartz, hematite or black tourmaline in between the feet to serve as an anchor.

How to Clear Your Crystals

Crystals have the ability to collect different types of energies from thoughts, touch, emotions, as well as from the environment itself. This means that when other people hold your crystals, they leave energy imprints which somehow change its purpose and intention. It is therefore important to learn how to clear your crystal so that you can use it just like new. Below are ways on how to clear your crystals from unnecessary energies.

- **Sea salt method:** Salt has the power to cleanse all things. Use sea salt for this method and bury the crystals in it overnight. Make sure that you place the salt in an inert container like a glass or ceramic. Once you are done clearing your crystals, wash off the salt with filtered water. This method is a bit harsh so make sure that you determine whether your crystals react negatively to salt.

- **Smudging:** Smudging is a technique of clearing crystals by using smoke from burnt sage and cedar leaves. Burn the dried leaves and pass your crystals through the smoke several times. This method is not only effective in clearing the crystals but also the body and environment.

- **Breathing:** Hold your crystals in your dominant hand and focus your thoughts and attention towards it. Your intention should focus on removing all negative energy in your crystal. Hold this thought and inhale through the nose. Exhale forcefully using your mouth. Your exhaled breath carries your positive intention to clear your crystals. Make sure that your intentions are strong otherwise this method will not be effective.

- **Charging:** Charging your crystals means revitalizing it with the energy that you want to be stored inside your crystals. You can do this by putting your crystals under direct sunlight or under the moon. You can also cluster them to form pyramids or bury them in snow or earth so that they absorb the energies of different positive matters.

Mind Programming

Once your crystals are cleared, you need to program them such that they will have energetic charge to them. Mind programming your crystals can also help you manifest your desires and dreams so that you can achieve them. Below are the steps on how to mind program your crystals.

- Hold the crystals in your hands and gaze at it. Do not lose the crystals from your sight.
- Take long deep breathes and concentrate on how you want to program your crystals. Think of your goals (good job, better relationship, and good health) and visualize the image in your mind.
- Exhale and send your desire to the crystals.
- You can always replace your intentions by repeating the steps.

Conclusion

Crystal healing is the hype of alternative medicine and it uses crystals to balance our chakras. It uses the powers of crystals to heal different disorders and align the spiritual, mental and physical bodies. It is a non-invasive way of treating people from their diseases with surprisingly great results. If you want achieve holistic treatment for your maladies, then you should include crystal healing in your daily routines.

Copyright © 2015. All rights reserved.

Except as permitted under the United States Copyright Act of 1976, reproduction or utilization of this work in any form or by any electronic, mechanical, or other means, now known or hereafter invented, including xerography, photocopying, and recording, and in any information storage and retrieval system, is forbidden without written permission.

The ideas, concepts, and opinions expressed in this book are intended to be used for educational and reference purposes only. Author and publisher claim no responsibility to any person or entity for any liability, loss, or damage caused or alleged to be caused directly or indirectly as a result of the use, application, or interpretation of the material in this book.

Printed in Great Britain
by Amazon